teacher's friend publications

Spring

a creative idea book for the elementary teacher

written and illustrated
by
Karen Sevaly

poems by
Margaret Bolz

Copyright © 1990
Teacher's Friend Publications, Inc.
All rights reserved.
Printed in the United States of America.
Published by Teacher's Friend Publications, Inc.
7407 Orangewood Drive, Riverside, CA 92504

ISBN 0-943263-16-6

THIS BOOK
IS DEDICATED
TO
TEACHERS AND CHILDREN
EVERYWHERE!

Table of Contents

Notes

Children are especially responsive to the various holidays and themes associated with the four seasons. Teacher's Friend has published the **"Spring"** Idea Book, to assist teachers in motivating students, with this in mind.

WHO USES THIS BOOK:

Preschool and elementary teachers along with Scout leaders, Sunday School teachers and parents all love the monthly and seasonal idea books.

Each idea or craft can easily be adapted to fit a wide range of grade levels. Kindergarteners can color and cut out the simple, bold patterns while older students love expanding these same patterns and crafts to a more complex format. Most of the ideas and activities are open-ended. Teachers may add their own curriculum appropriate for the grade level they teach. Young children may practice number, color or letter recognition while older students may like to drill multiplication facts or match homonyms.

WHAT YOU'LL FIND IN THIS BOOK:

Teachers and parents will find a variety of crafts, activities, bulletin board ideas and patterns that compliment the monthly holidays and seasonal themes. Children will be delighted with the booklet covers, bingo cards, name tags, mobiles, place cards, writing pages and gameboards. There is also a special section devoted to the sport of the season!

HOW TO USE THIS BOOK:

Every page of this book may be duplicated for individual classroom use. Some pages are meant to be used as duplicating masters or student worksheets. Most of the crafts and patterns may be copied onto construction paper or printed on index paper. Children can then make the crafts by cutting them out and coloring them with crayons or colored markers.

Many of the pages can be enlarged with an overhead or opaque projector. The patterns can then be used for door displays, bulletin boards or murals.

MOBILES:

Making mobiles are especially fun for all ages. Teachers may like to simplify mobile construction for younger children by using one of these ideas.

DRINKING STRAW MOBILE - Thread a piece of yarn through a plastic drinking straw and tie a mobile pattern to each end. Flatten a paper clip and bend it around the center of the straw for hanging. The mobile can easily be balanced by adjusting the yarn. (Older students can make their mobiles the same way but may wish to add additional levels by hanging other mobiles directly below the first.)

CLOTHES HANGER MOBILE - Mobiles can easily be made with a wire clothes hanger, as shown. Just tie each pattern piece to the hanger with thread, yarn or kite string.

YARN MOBILE - The most simple mobile is made by gluing the pattern pieces to a length of yarn, each piece spaced directly beneath the other. Tie a bow at the top and hang in a window or from the ceiling.

CLIP ART PAGES:

The illustrations on these pages may be used in classroom bulletins, newspapers, notes home or just to decorate your own worksheets. Cut the illustrations out and paste them to your originals before printing. The drawings may be enlarged or reduced on some copy machines. You are also free to enlarge the characters for other uses, such as; bulletin boards, calendar decorations, booklet covers and awards.

PLACE CARDS OR NAME TAGS:

If possible, laminate the finished name tags or place cards. Use a special dry transfer marker or dark crayon to write the names on the laminated surface. After the special day, simply wipe off the letters with a tissue for use at another time.

POETRY:

Children love clever poems. Use the poems in this book to inspire your students and at the same time record the improvement in their handwriting.

Each morning, copy one or two lines, or an entire poem, on the class chalkboard. Ask the children to copy it in their best handwriting. Have them write the date at the top of the page. The children can then collect the poems chronologically in a notebook. This is a great way to show parents how their child's handwriting has improved.

STAND-UP CHARACTERS:

All of the stand-up characters in this book can easily be made from construction or index paper. Children can add the color and cut them out. The characters can be used as table decorations, name cards or used in a puppet show. Several characters can also be joined at the hands, as shown.

The characters can also be enlarged on posterboard for a bulletin board display or reduced in size for use in a diorama or as finger puppets.

BULLETIN BOARDS:

Creating clever bulletin boards can be a fun experience for you and your students. Many of the bulletin board ideas in this book contain patterns that the students can make themselves. You simply need to cover the board with bright paper, (preferably only once a year) and display the appropriate heading. Students make their own pumpkins for a classroom pumpkin patch or creative writing apples for a Johnny Appleseed display.

Many of the illustrations in this book can also be enlarged and displayed on a bulletin board. Use an over-head or opaque projector to do your enlargements. When you enlarge a character, think BIG! Figures three, four or even five feet tall can make a dramatic display. Use colored butcher paper for large displays eliminating the need to add color with markers or crayons.

WHATEVER YOU DO....

Have fun using the ideas in this book. Be creative! Develop your own ideas and adapt the patterns and crafts to fit your own curriculum. By using your imagination, you will be encouraging your students to be more creative. A creative classroom is a fun classroom! One that promotes an enthusiasm for learning!

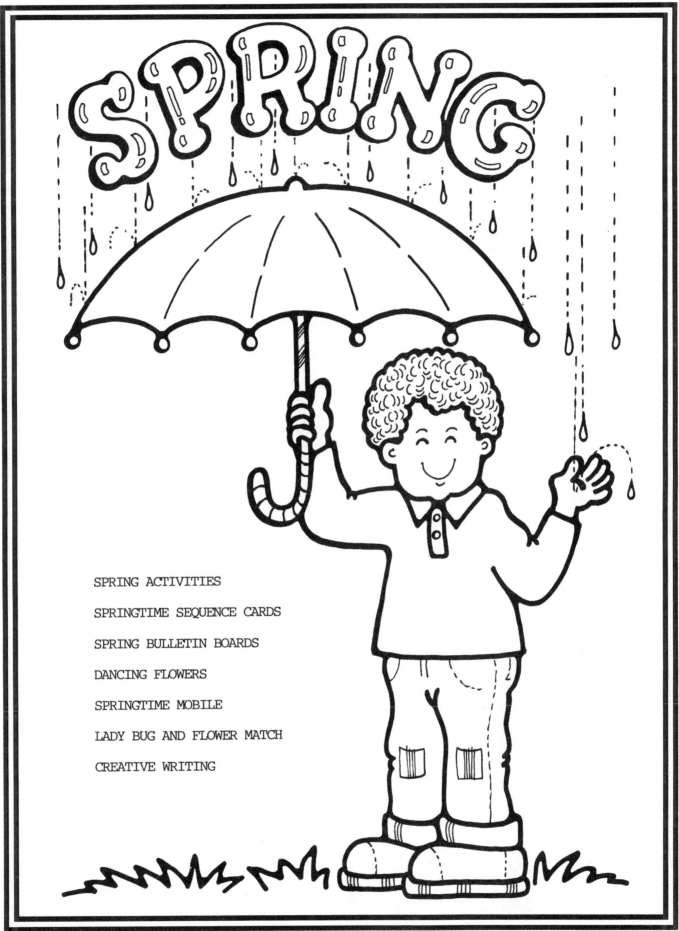

SPRING

SPRING ACTIVITIES

SPRINGTIME SEQUENCE CARDS

SPRING BULLETIN BOARDS

DANCING FLOWERS

SPRINGTIME MOBILE

LADY BUG AND FLOWER MATCH

CREATIVE WRITING

Springtime Activities

SPRING RAIN

Grab your umbrella, hold tight and stay under.
A cloudburst brings rain and lightning and thunder.
An umbrella in spring, you should never forget.
For one thing is certain, rain always is wet.

SPRINGTIME GARDENS

As part of your science program, ask students to plant a variety of springtime gardens!

One suggestion might be to have students use an old aquarium, turning it into a plant terrarium. Use a planting mix purchased from a local nursery and ask students to plant seeds or small plants. They may like to keep records of the daily care and the growth of each plant.

Many different types of seeds can successfully be sprouted in egg cartons. Make sure that you punch a hole in the bottom of each compartment for drainage, if you use styrofoam cartons. Place the cartons in a sunny window and have your students observe which type of seeds grow most quickly.

You might even like to sprout avacado seeds or sweet potatoes in water. Alfalfa seeds, also, sprout beautifully in the classroom and can later be added to students' lunchtime sandwiches.

Spring Bingo

This game offers an exciting way to introduce students to the spring season. Give each child a copy of the bingo words listed below or write the words on the chalkboard. Ask students to write any 24 words on his or her bingo card. Use the same directions you might use for regular bingo.

SPRING	WEATHER	GREEN	ARBOR DAY
MARCH	WINDY	POT OF GOLD	TREES
APRIL	KITE	EASTER	MOTHER'S DAY
MAY	RAINY	EGGS	GIFTS
FLOWERS	UMBRELLA	HATCH	MAY DAY
COLORFUL	RAINBOW	BASKET	MEMORIAL DAY
BLOOM	SUNSHINE	BUNNY	BUTTERFLIES
BUD	SAINT PATRICK	GRASS	BUGS
LEAVES	SHAMROCK	APRIL FOOLS	BEES
GROW	LEPRECHAUN	JOKES	INSECTS

SPRING BINGO

FREE

SPRING NEWS
A NOTE HOME TO PARENTS

Springtime Sequence Cards

Spring Bulletin Boards

SOARING HIGH!

Display a large paper kite on the class bulletin board to encourage and motivate your students in specific areas. As each student accomplishes a required task, reward them with their own kite bow. Children love seeing their names prominately displayed.

This easy idea can also be used to introduce new vocabulary words, mathematical concepts or as a way to welcome students to class that first day!

POINT OUT THE BEST!

Emphasize the importance of weekly or daily lessons by "pointing" it out to your students! By using the pattern on the next page, you can "point" out important calendar events, classroom monitors, or the letter or color of the week. Children will love assisting you in changing the board to the appropriate area.

TIME TO BLOOM!

Most classroom clocks have a round face, perfect for the center of a large paper flower! Cut a circle, the size of your clock face, in the center of a piece of poster board. Cut large paper petals and leaves from colored construction paper and staple them around the hole. Glue bits of fluffy tissue paper to the edge of the cut circle and place the entire flower over the face of your clock. What an easy, colorful way to celebrate the blooming of spring!

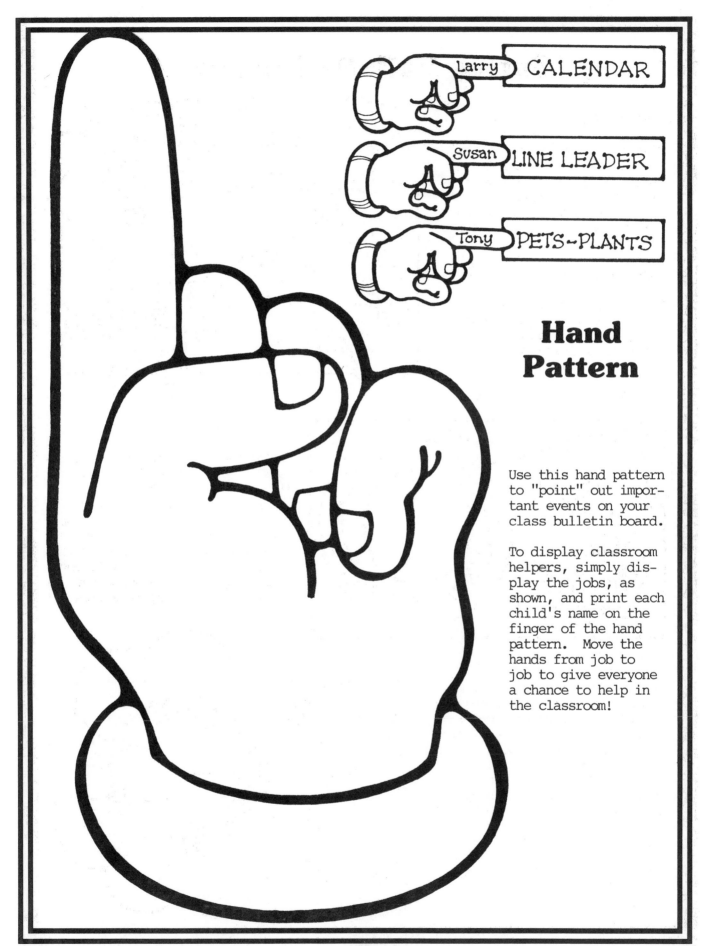

Larry — CALENDAR

Susan — LINE LEADER

Tony — PETS~PLANTS

Hand Pattern

Use this hand pattern to "point" out important events on your class bulletin board.

To display classroom helpers, simply display the jobs, as shown, and print each child's name on the finger of the hand pattern. Move the hands from job to job to give everyone a chance to help in the classroom!

Kite Pattern

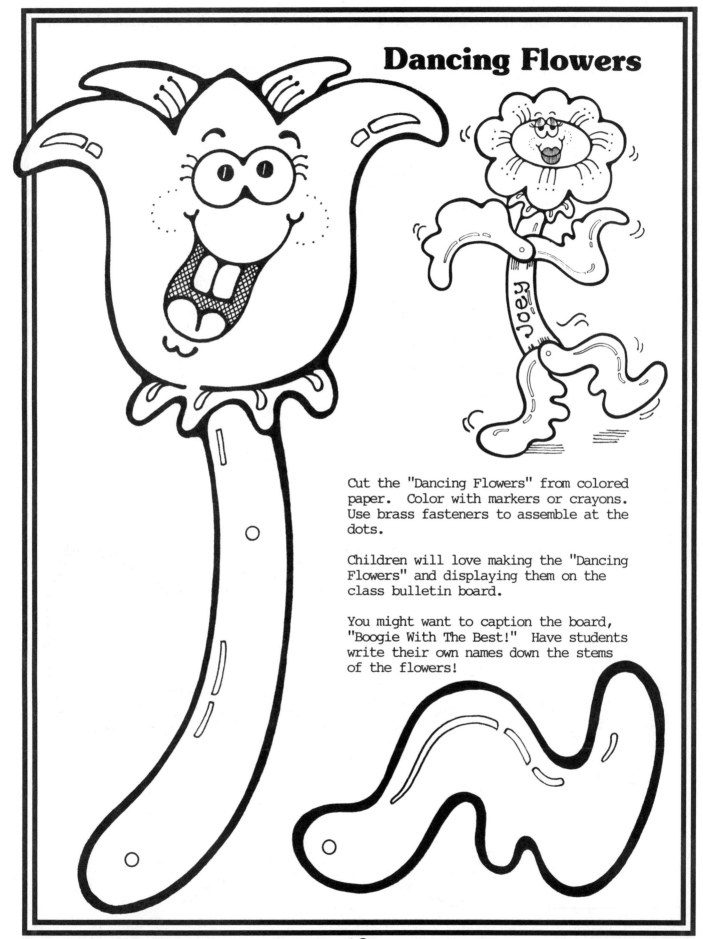

Cut the "Dancing Flowers" from colored paper. Color with markers or crayons. Use brass fasteners to assemble at the dots.

Children will love making the "Dancing Flowers" and displaying them on the class bulletin board.

You might want to caption the board, "Boogie With The Best!" Have students write their own names down the stems of the flowers!

Springtime Mobile

Each student can make his own "Springtime Mobile" using these simple patterns. Cut the patterns from index or construction paper and assemble with thread or yarn, as shown.

Children might like to draw their own flowers for the mobile or add more than two raindrops.

Umbrella Pattern

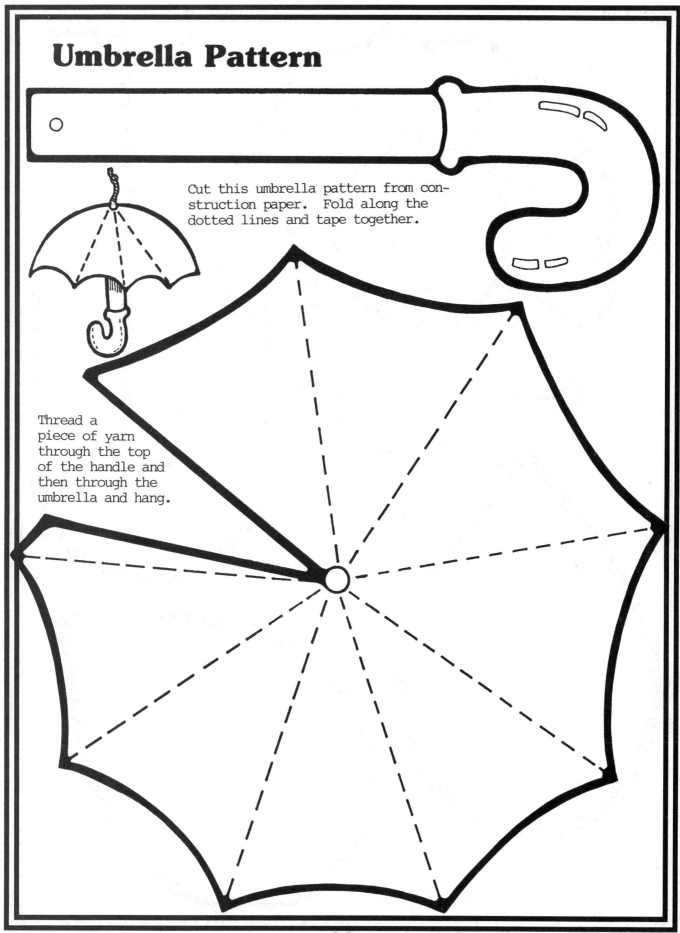

Cut this umbrella pattern from construction paper. Fold along the dotted lines and tape together.

Thread a piece of yarn through the top of the handle and then through the umbrella and hang.

Stained Glass Butterflies

These "Stained Glass Pictures" are strikingly beautiful and simple to make.

You will need the following materials:

Several permanent colored markers   Black construction paper
Plastic food-storage wrap   Tape
Aluminum foil   8" paper plates

Tape the butterfly patterns to a smooth desk top. Ask each child to stretch a piece of plastic wrap over the pattern of their choice and tape in place. The child colors the picture using the colored markers. When the picture is complete, ask the student to trace all of the black lines using a black permanent marker.

The next step is to have the student take a square of foil, measuring one foot, and crumple it carefully. The student then spreads the foil over a paper plate, taping it in place. Now, the student takes his finished picture, on the plastic wrap, and tapes it over the foil. Mount the entire project on black construction paper and hang in a window or display on the class bulletin board.

Lady Bug and Flower Match

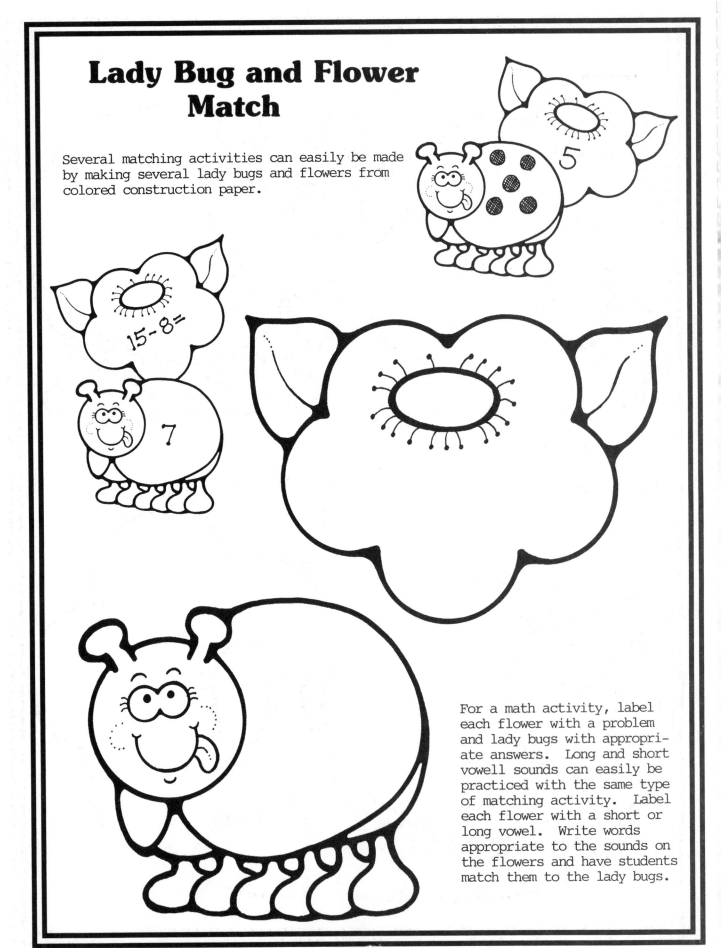

Several matching activities can easily be made by making several lady bugs and flowers from colored construction paper.

15 - 8 =

For a math activity, label each flower with a problem and lady bugs with appropriate answers. Long and short vowell sounds can easily be practiced with the same type of matching activity. Label each flower with a short or long vowel. Write words appropriate to the sounds on the flowers and have students match them to the lady bugs.

27

Flower Power

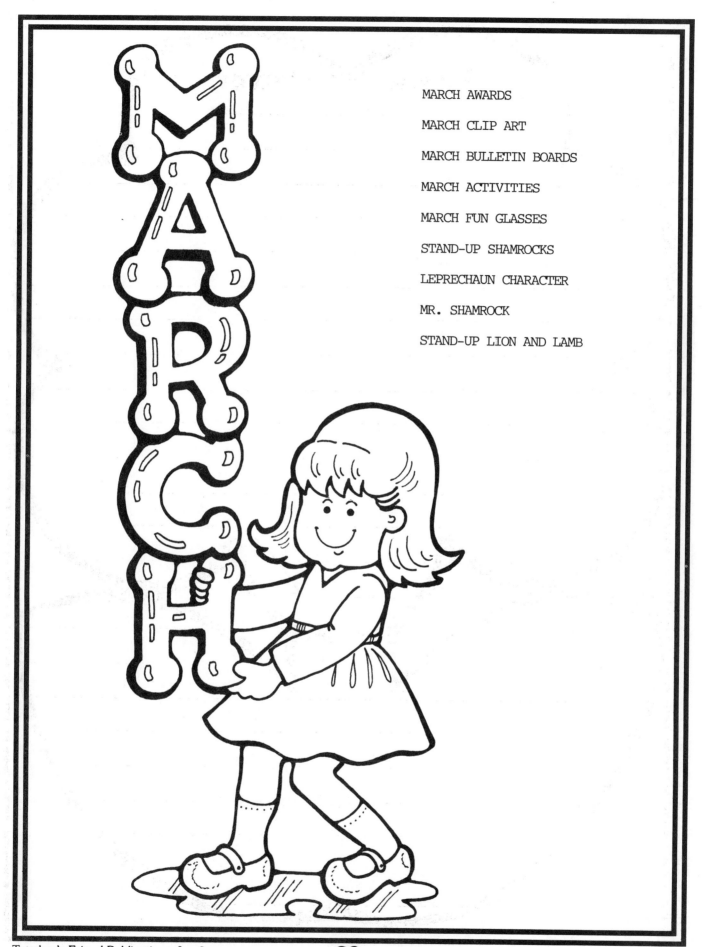

MARCH AWARDS

MARCH CLIP ART

MARCH BULLETIN BOARDS

MARCH ACTIVITIES

MARCH FUN GLASSES

STAND-UP SHAMROCKS

LEPRECHAUN CHARACTER

MR. SHAMROCK

STAND-UP LION AND LAMB

SUPER STUDENT AWARD!

awarded to

_____

for

_____

_____

_____

_____
Date

_____
Teacher

STUDENT OF THE MONTH

AWARDED TO

_____
Name

_____

_____

_____
Teacher

_____
Date

Type the name of your school, address and telephone number in this space. Include your name and room number, also.

Suggestions for a March newsletter:

List the name of each student that was selected student of the week for the month of February.

Note the special days of the month, such as Saint Patrick's Day. (Make sure that parents know which days children will not be in attendance if spring vacation falls within this month.)

Announce special programs or activities being conducted by your school or in your classroom.

Tell about something special your class is currently working on.

Staple the March cafeteria menu to each newsletter.

Ask one of your students to draw several small pictures about Saint Patrick's Day to be used in the March newsletter.

Ask your school principal to write a brief message that can be included with the March newsletter.

Ask for parent volunteers or donations for the class Saint Patrick's Day party. (Easter may also fall during the month of March.)

Announce upcoming field trips, class plays or fund raisers.

Send a welcome note to a new student or a get well message to a student that has been out ill.

March Bulletin Boards

HATS OFF!

Portray the winds of March by displaying flying hats across the class bulletin board. Children can bring hats from home to display or have them make the hats from the patterns found in this book. Add feathers, buttons, fabric and other novelties for decorations.

GENTLE AS LAMBS

What a great way to emphasize the many ways we should be acting at school and at home! Display a large lamb on the board. Add cotton balls for a fluffy effect. With the help of your students, list the various qualities that make each of us a happier, nicer person.

WE ARE GENTLE AS LAMBS!

SHARE WITH OTHERS!

BE FRIENDLY!

BE HELPFUL!   BE HONEST!

BE KIND!   BE PATIENT!

RESPECT OTHERS' PROPERTY!

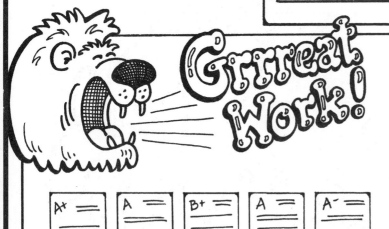

GREAT WORK!

Emphasize the greatness of good classroom work by displaying this roaring lion! Children might also like to write papers about things they find "Grrrrreat!"

Roaring Lion

Gentle Lamb

Hat Booklet

Children will love using this hat pattern to write creative stories about the wind or even fashion design. Students might like to decorate their hats with sequins, feathers or cut-paper flowers. Display the hats on the class bulletin board.

Hats

March Activities

GREEN, GREEN!
Celebrate Saint Patrick's Day by providing a tasty treat for your students!

Green bell peppers offer an excellent source of vitamins and minerals. Along with generous amounts of ranch dressing, your students will gobble them up.

Bell peppers also provide an excellent way to stamp attractive shamrocks. Cut the pepper in half, side-ways, and clean out any seeds from the inside. Using green paint, dip in the pepper and stamp the "Pepper Shamrock" onto white paper.

This is a great activity to introduce young children to a new vegetable!

MARCH BEGINNINGS

March is when the earth's renewed,
A very pleasant interlude.
A new beginning bursts all over.
Everything turns green as clover.
March wind replaced by gentle breeze,
Flowers bloom and so do bees.
March is like a great invention,
But, springtime sports get my attention!

WINDY ACTIVITIES

When the March winds blow, ask your students to try some of these fun suggestions:

Make paper airplanes and see which one flies farthest.

Have a balloon launch with messages inside.

Make kites from paper lunch sacks and fly them during physical education or recess.

Make frisbees from disposable plastic plates. Children can decorate them with permanent colored markers.

Make your own bubble wands from plastic six-pack holders. See who can get the most bubbles in the air at one time.

(A great bubble mixture can be made by using $\frac{1}{2}$ cup of liquid detergent, 1 quart of water and a couple of tablespoons of white Karo syrup. Refrigerate overnight before using.)

March Fun Glasses

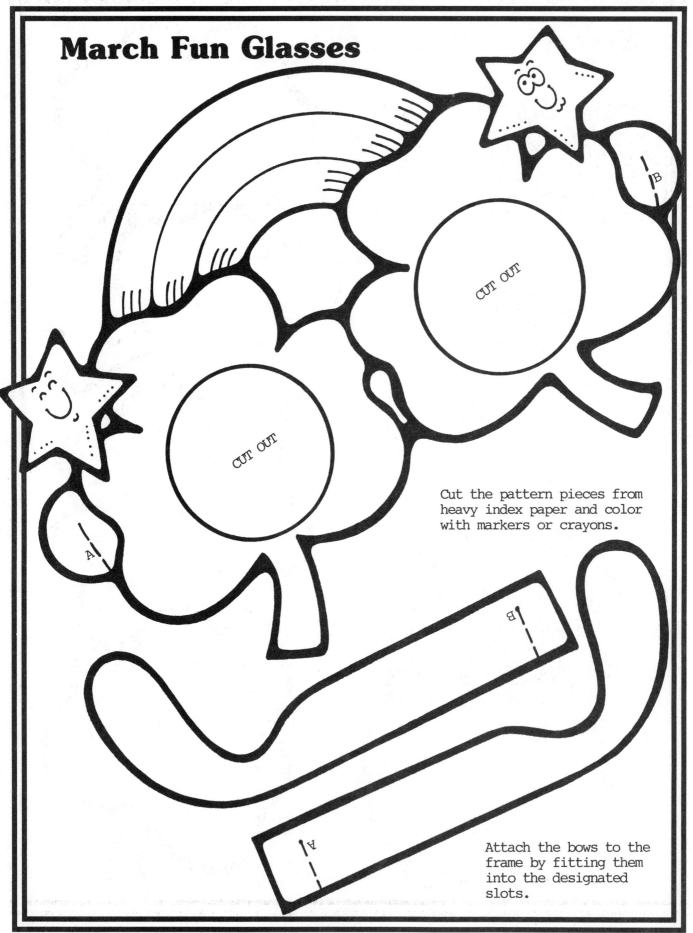

CUT OUT

CUT OUT

Cut the pattern pieces from
heavy index paper and color
with markers or crayons.

Attach the bows to the
frame by fitting them
into the designated
slots.

Stand-Up Shamrocks

Cut out the pot of gold and shamrocks from heavy paper. Children can write their own springtime messages or names across the shamrocks. Fan-fold along the dotted lines. Glue the pot of gold to the first shamrock and stand on a desk top for a March decoration.

Good as Gold!

JACK

Leprechaun Character

Make this cute Leprechaun character from index paper. Color, cut out and fold. Bend his arms forward and staple or paste the pot of gold to his hands.

Use as a table decoration for Saint Patrick's Day!

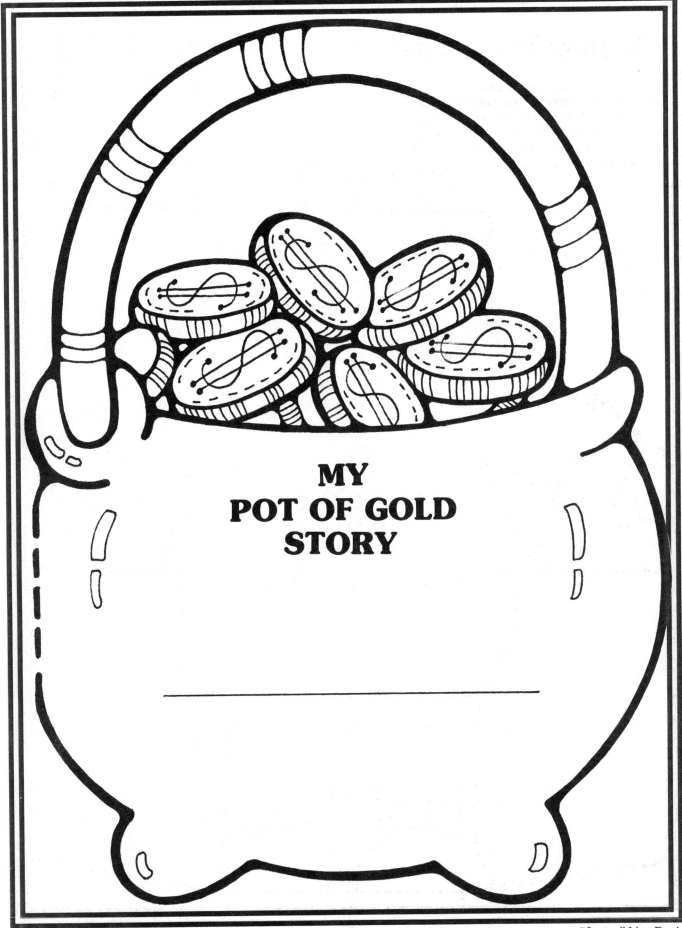

MY
POT OF GOLD
STORY

_____

Mr.
Shamrock

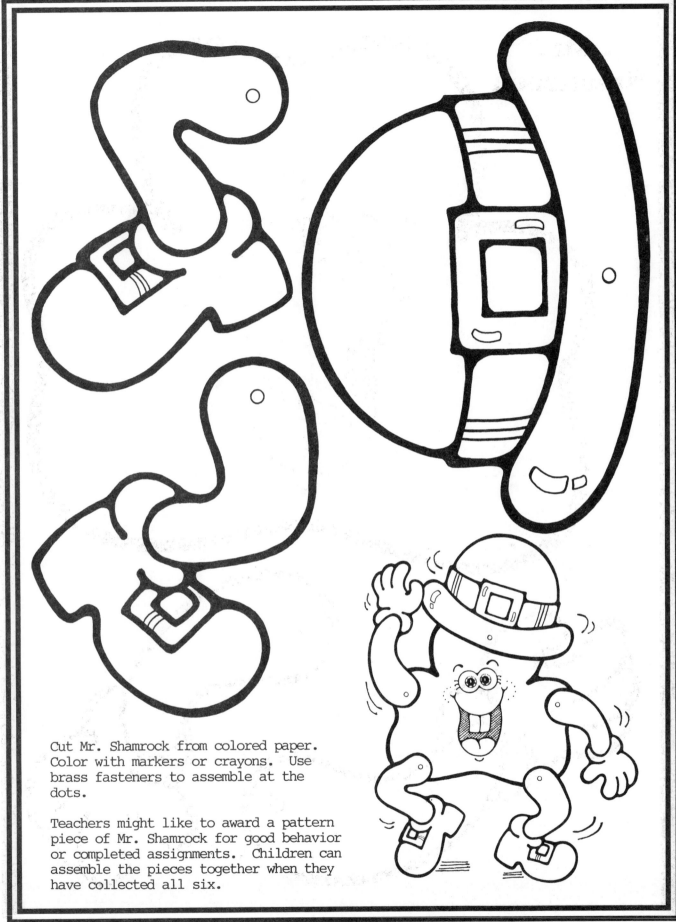

Cut Mr. Shamrock from colored paper.
Color with markers or crayons. Use
brass fasteners to assemble at the
dots.

Teachers might like to award a pattern
piece of Mr. Shamrock for good behavior
or completed assignments. Children can
assemble the pieces together when they
have collected all six.

Stand-Up Lion

Make this Stand-Up Lion from index or construction paper. Color, cut and fold. Fold his legs forward, along the dotted lines. Curl his tail around a pencil and fold to the back. Stand the Lion and the Lamb on a table to celebrate the coming of spring!

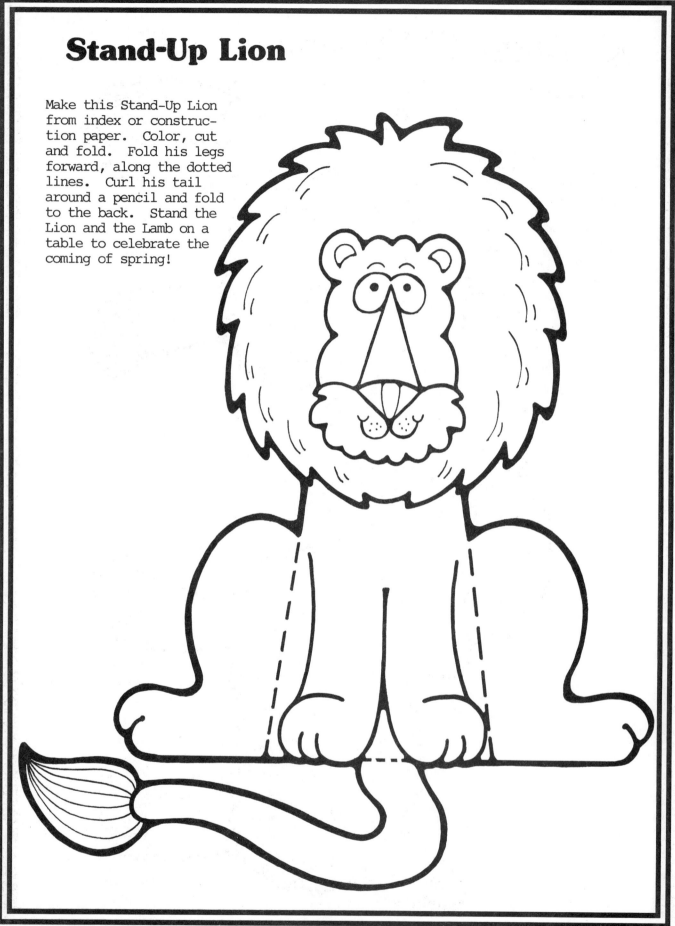

Stand-Up Lamb

Make this Stand-Up Lamb from index or construction paper. Color, cut and fold.

You may want to glue white cotton balls to your lamb for a fluffy effect!

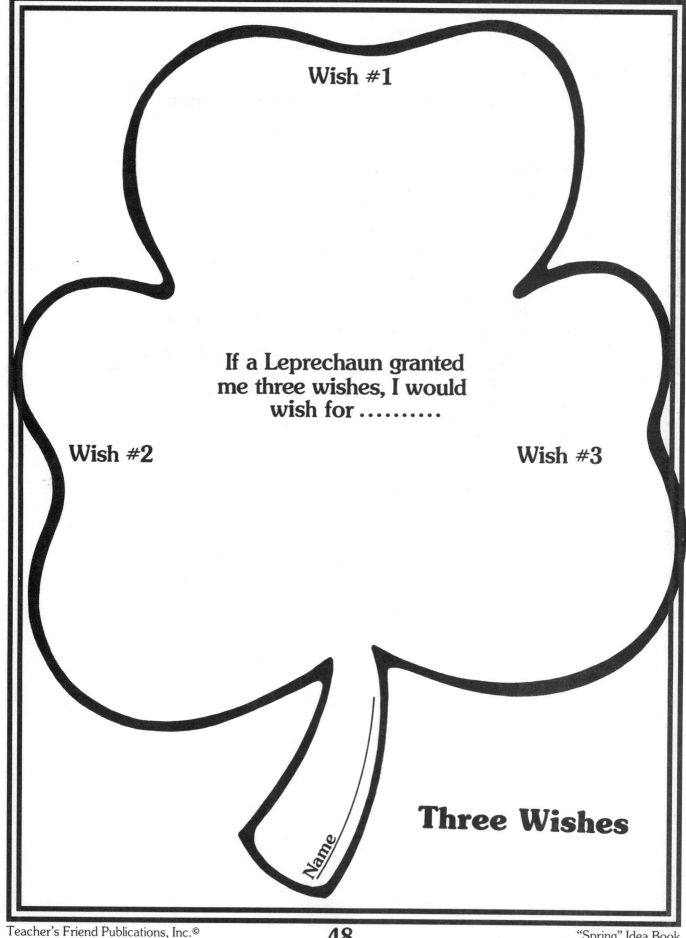

Wish #1

If a Leprechaun granted me three wishes, I would wish for ....

Wish #2   Wish #3

Name

Three Wishes

SUPER STUDENT AWARD!

awarded to

_____

for

_____

_____

_____

_____
Date

_____
Teacher

STUDENT OF THE MONTH
AWARDED TO

_____
Name

_____

_____

_____
Teacher

_____
Date

Type the name of your school, address and telephone number in this space. Include your name and room number, also.

Suggestions for an April newsletter:

List the name of each student that was selected student of the week for the month of April.

Note the dates of spring vacation and Easter. Make sure that parents know which days children will not be in attendance.

Announce special activities or programs being conducted by your school or in your classroom.

Tell about something special your class is currently working on.

Staple the April cafeteria menu to each newsletter.

Ask one of your students to draw several small pictures about Easter to be used in the April newsletter.

Ask your school principal to write a brief message that can be included with the April newsletter.

Ask for parent volunteers or donations for the class Easter party or egg hunt.

Announce upcoming field trips, class plays, sport activities or fund raisers.

Send a welcome note to a new student or a get well message to a student that has been out ill.

Include a joke or riddle in celebration of April Fool's Day.

April Clip Art

April Bulletin Boards

LOOK WHAT'S HATCHING!

This goofy hatching chick will make your students giggle with delight!

Display him on the class bulletin board along with creative writing egg booklets made by your students. The egg booklets can de decorated with crayons or markers to resemble Easter eggs.

SWINGING BUNNY!

Enlarge this cute bunny and display him on the class door or bulletin board. Glue on fluffy white cotton for his tail and use real rope or cording for the swing ropes. A cute title might be, "Swing Into Spring!"

COLOR YOUR WORLD.....

Fluffy white clouds cut from polyester batting sets off this colorful spring bulletin board. Various colors of twisted crepe paper strips form the rainbow. Children can write colorful poems that can be displayed around the board.

Hatching Stories

Swinging Bunny

April Activities

APRIL

Depending on the tide and moon,
Easter may come late or soon,
In March or April, it changes around.
More often in April, it is found.

April Fool is the very first day.
On one another tricks we play.
April is beautiful with cool grass and flowers
I wish it were longer by days and by hours.

Try these springtime activities:

DAYLIGHT-SAVING TIME

It's time to "spring" forward with daylight-saving time! Set your clocks one hour ahead of standard time and ask your students to observe the lengthening days. Students can chart the daylight hours by checking the daily newspaper for the time of each sunrise and sunset. Using a large graph, have them note these times. Draw lines from dot to dot to illustrate how the daylight hours are increasing.

FREE TIME "EGGS"TRAVAGANZA

Bring a large Easter basket to school full of colorful plastic Easter eggs. As each student finishes his or her work, they are free to select an egg and do whatever is instructed on the slip of paper hidden inside. Some suggestions might be; "Make an Easter card for mom and dad," or, "Be the first excused at the next recess!"

Children will be eager to complete the days work when such a fun Easter surprise awaits them!

EASTER EGGS

My Easter basket has inside
Easter eggs that have been dyed,

Pretty eggs the chickens laid,
Decorated and displayed.

Boiled eggs in soft pastels
And pictures painted on the shells.

Like rainbow colors in the sky,
So are the colors in the dye.

Every year this great tradition
Leaves me with a firm decision.

Although egg dyeing is great fun,
Afterwards, to eat each one.

Eating Easter eggs I peel,
Day after day, for many a meal.

This decision can't be truer,
"Maybe, next year, I'll dye fewer."

April Fun Glasses

Cut the pattern pieces from heavy index paper and color with markers or crayons. Attach the bows to frame by fitting them into the designated slots.

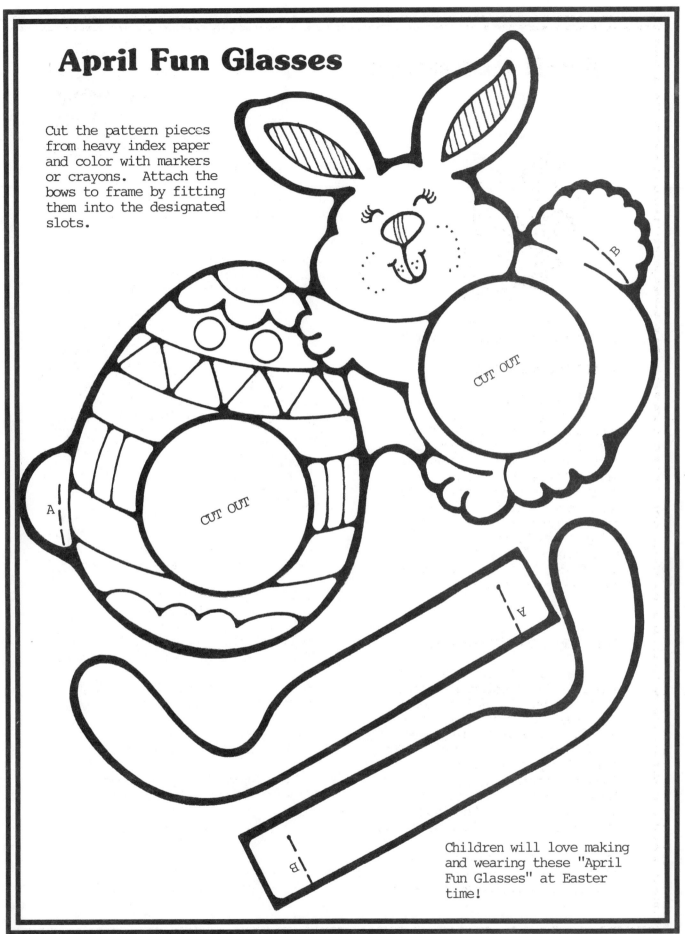

Children will love making and wearing these "April Fun Glasses" at Easter time!

Stand-Up Easter Eggs

Cut the Easter eggs and bunny from heavy paper. Write your own Easter message across the eggs. Fan fold along the dotted lines. Glue the bunny to the first egg and stand on a desk top for a Easter decoration.

MY BUNNY BOOK

Stand-Up Bunny

Make this cute bunny character from index paper. Color, cut out and fold. Bend his arms forward and staple or paste the basket to his hands.

Bunny Mask and Ears

Cut this cute bunny mask and ears pattern from colored construction paper. Glue the ears to the top of the mask, as shown. Students might like to add pipe cleaner whiskers to the bunny mask. Tie the mask to the back of the head with heavy kite string.

These bunny ears can also be attached to a paper headband and worn by children during the annual Easter egg hunt.

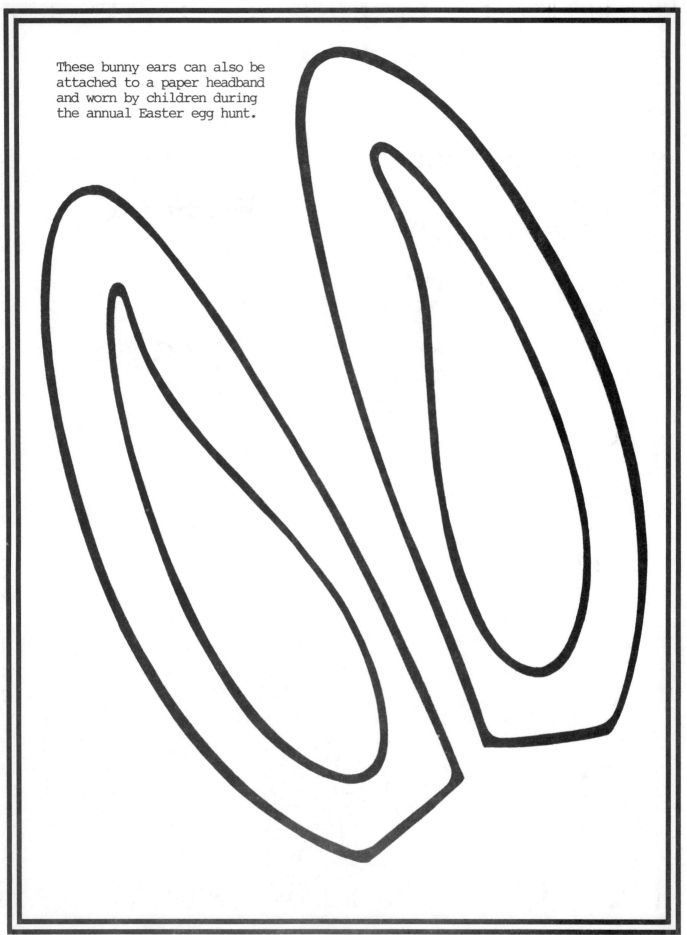

Egg Holders

Cut these egg holders from heavy index or construction paper. Color with crayons or markers. Write your own springtime or Easter message on either side of the character. Glue or staple the two ends together to form a loop and stand a hard-boiled Easter egg inside. This is a cute way to display your decorated eggs during this spring holiday!

These holders can also be used as Easter napkin rings for your holiday dinner table!

Your students might enjoy coloring Easter eggs in the classroom. Try some of these unusual ways of dyeing eggs:

Soak various colors of crepe paper in small cups of hot water. Dye the eggs the same way you would using a commercial egg dye.

A small flower or leaf can be placed on the egg shell and then wrapped tightly with a nylon stocking. After dyeing, remove the nylon and leaf to reveal a beautiful, natural design!

Wrap your eggs with rubber-bands and then dye them. Remove the rubber bands to reveal the interesting designs.

Use vegetables to dye your eggs! Spinach or onion skins boiled on a stove top, work very well. You might, also, want to experiment with teabags or beets!

NAME

APRIL SHOWERS
BRING MAY FLOWERS

April Showers Bring May Flowers Mobile

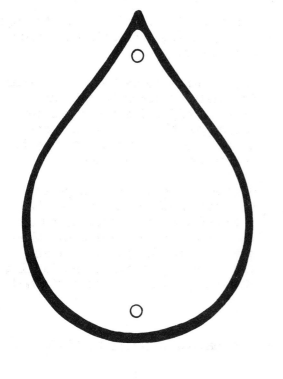

Each child can make his or her own "April Showers Mobile" by cutting these pattern pieces from colored construction paper. (They may want to mount the finished pieces on poster board for added durability.)

Children can write spring vocabulary words on the pattern pieces.

April Fool's Day Activities

April is National Humor month, a perfect time to explore the funny world in which we live. (Remember, April 1st is April Fool's Day!)

Suggest some of these "funny" activities to your students:

FUNNY PAPERS

Start a collection of comic strips on the class bulletin board. Ask children to gather cartoons and comic strips found in magazines and newspapers. They may also like to write and draw their own cartoons that can be featured on the board. Soon your bulletin board will be filled with a variety of funny illustrations, guaranteed to liven up any school day!

COMEDY HOUR

Children will love being in the spot light, acting out their own jokes and riddles.

Ask students to gather their favorite skits or jokes to act out. (They should write the jokes out before performing them in front of the class.) Encourage them to use props, if they like.

Make a microphone from a paper tube and black yarn. Darken the room and put your class comedian in a spotlight (flashlight), when he or she performs. The class can act as an audience, applauding after each comedian has performed.

APRIL FOOL'S ELF

Delight your students on the first of April by having an April Fool's Elf visit the classroom!

When students arrive that morning, they each find a part of a secret message taped to the top of his or her desk. (Write the entire message on a large sheet of butcher paper. Cut the message into sections, numbering each one for easier deciphering.) Have the students arrange the messages in order and read the entire secret message out loud. This message can tell students cute things about themselves. Or, have the elf ask them to do particular activities during the day, such as; drawing pictures of the elf, writing letters or cleaning out their desks. Later in the day, another message can be left, directing them to a special ice cream treat!

You might want to extend the elf's visit for several days. His presence can be used to motivate children with better behavior or improved study skills. Make sure to take care that the students never suspect that you are the April Fool's Elf!

This fun activity can also be used on March 17th, Saint Patrick's Day. Simply change the elf to a leprechaun!

My Favorite April Fool's Joke

Did you hear the one about...

MY JOKE BOOK

Name

Arbor Day Activities

Arbor Day comes at different times of the year in different parts of the world. The first Arbor Day, in the United States, was celebrated in the state of Nebraska on April 22, 1872. Many states followed suit, celebrating Arbor Day in the month of April.

On Arbor Day, many schools and civic organizations plant one or more trees to beautify their parks and cities. In some countries, Arbor Day comes when a child is born. The family plants a tree and names it after the baby. Some people plant one kind of tree for a girl and another for a boy.

Here are some activities that can be used to help recognize Arbor Day:

1. COLLECTION OF LEAVES - Ask children to collect unusual leaves from a variety of trees. They can display the leaves on the class bulletin board and categorize them according to the type of tree; such as, deciduous, evergreen, etc.

   They could also use the leaves for crayon rubbings. Place the leaves on a smooth desk top and have students lay a piece of plain paper on top of the leaves. Children gently crayon over the leaves creating interesting designs and textures from the various leaf shapes.

2. TREE QUESTIONS - Hold a class discussion regarding the various types of trees and the purpose they serve in our world. Here are a few questions you might want to use to start off your discussion.

   Trees are important because they provide oxygen. Why is this important? Where in the world are people most concerned about the depletion of our forests? What reasons do they give?

   Trees are used in various industries. What products are made from trees? What type of trees are used? What type of jobs rely on tree products?

   How can we preserve our forests? What steps can we take to recycle wood products? What alternatives are available?

3. RESEARCH TREES - Assign each student a type of tree to research. They might like to include a drawing of their tree, explain it's seasonal changes and list it's various functions and purposes.

   You might want to assign a state to each child in the class. Have students research their state's official tree. Drawings of the trees can be displayed around a map of the United States. Yarn can be used to indicate which tree belongs to which state.

My Tree

Name of my tree

_____

My tree is....

Evergreen ☐

Deciduous ☐

Hardwood ☐

Softwood ☐

Where my tree grows _____
_____
_____
_____

Products made from my tree
_____
_____
_____

My tree drawing

_____
_____

leaf drawing

bark drawing

Some interesting things about my tree _____
_____
_____
_____

What I like best about my tree _____
_____

My Tree Report

MAY AWARDS

MAY CLIP ART

MAY ACTIVITIES

MAY BULLETIN BOARDS

MAY FUN GLASSES

STAND-UP FLOWERS

MOTHER'S DAY ACTIVITIES

STAND-UP MOM

MAKE MOM HAPPY GAME

MOTHER'S DAY COUPON BOOK

SUPER STUDENT AWARD!

awarded to

_____

for

_____
_____
_____

_____
Date

_____
Teacher

STUDENT OF THE MONTH
AWARDED TO

_____
Name

_____
_____

_____
Teacher

_____
Date

Type the name of your school, address and telephone number in this space. Include your name and room number, also.

Suggestions for a May newsletter:

List the name of each student that was selected student of the week for the month of April.

Note the dates of Mother's Day and Memorial Day. Make sure that parents know which days children will not be in attendance.

Announce special programs or activities being conducted by your school or in your classroom.

Tell about something special your class is currently working on.

Staple the May cafeteria menu to each newsletter.

Ask one of your students to draw several small pictures about springtime or Mother's Day to be used in the May newsletter.

Invite mothers to your classroom for a special Mother's Day tea.

Ask your school principal to write a brief message that can be included with the May newsletter.

Announce upcoming field trips, fund raisers or testing dates.

Send a welcome note to a new student or a get well message to a student that has been out ill.

May Clip Art

May Activities

MAY

The end of May is often good weather,
For families and friends to get together.
Picnic with a lunch mother made
Or sit on a curb to watch a parade.

Go to the beach for a swim and some fun
Or watch a ballgame or play in one.
Memorial Day, near the end of spring
To use as you choose, anyway, anything.

And so some people choose this day
To honor those who've passed away.
This day is for the entire nation.
No school. No work. A day of vacation.

CLASS FLOWER AND PLANT SHOW

A fun way to stimulate your students' interest and appreciation of May flowers
is to arrange for a class flower and plant show.

Familiarize your students with common garden plants by using encyclopedias,
seed catalogs and gardening books. You might like to ask a local gardener or
horticulturist to visit your class and talk about his or her hobby or profes-
sion. Children grow their flowers and plants at home and bring them to class
on the special day.

Divide the show into several categories. Categories might include plants
grown from seeds, fruits and vegetables, potted plants or flower arrangements.
Ask students to draw posters and invitations announcing the show and post them
around the school. (You might want to plan a date close to Mother's Day and
encourage all mothers to come share in the experience.) On the day of the show,
children vote for their favorite entry. Winners receive a special certificate
or ribbon.

CINCO DE MAYO - May 5th

Cinco De Mayo is a wonderful time to
teach students a little about Mexico.

As part of your celebrations, make a
colorful piñata with your students.
Place two or three large grocery bags
inside one another and fill with special treats. The children can add the
decorations. Hang the piñata with a
heavy cord and have students take turns
breaking it with a broom stick.

CINCO DE MAYO

Dancing feet and clapping hands,
Dance to Mariachi bands.
Violins play, trumpets blow,
Festive day of Mexico.

Cinco de Mayo, day of fun,
Food and drink for everyone.
Next year I'll come back for more,
Señorita and Señor!

May Bulletin Boards

FLY AWAY

These cute birds will fly across the class bulletin board to reach their goal of the bird house. Give each child a bird cut from colored paper. As books are read or assignments completed, the birds fly toward their goal. Each bird, or child, who reaches the bird house should be awarded with a special treat.

MERRY MAY MURAL

Cover a large bulletin board with blue butcher paper and divide your class into at least five groups. Give each group one phase of the mural to complete. Sky and clouds, trees, flowers, butterflies and birds, plus the title, are a few suggestions.

GROW WITH US!

Display a large potted plant made from construction paper on the classroom door or bulletin board. Children draw self portraits on small paper plates that are decorated as flowers. Arrange the flowers on the plant as a happy way to welcome everyone to your classroom!

Blooming Flowers

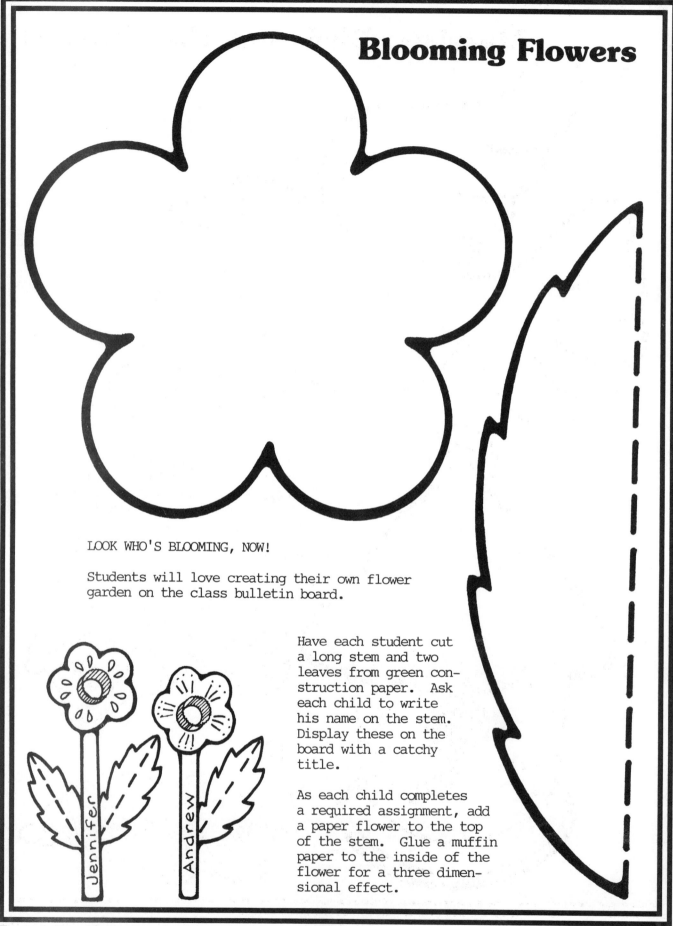

LOOK WHO'S BLOOMING, NOW!

Students will love creating their own flower
garden on the class bulletin board.

Have each student cut
a long stem and two
leaves from green con-
struction paper. Ask
each child to write
his name on the stem.
Display these on the
board with a catchy
title.

As each child completes
a required assignment, add
a paper flower to the top
of the stem. Glue a muffin
paper to the inside of the
flower for a three dimen-
sional effect.

Matching Birds and Bird Houses

Make several copies of birds and bird houses from colored construction paper. Use them in a variety of matching activities such as, letter recognition, math facts, words and definitions, opposites and so on.

Bird Mobile

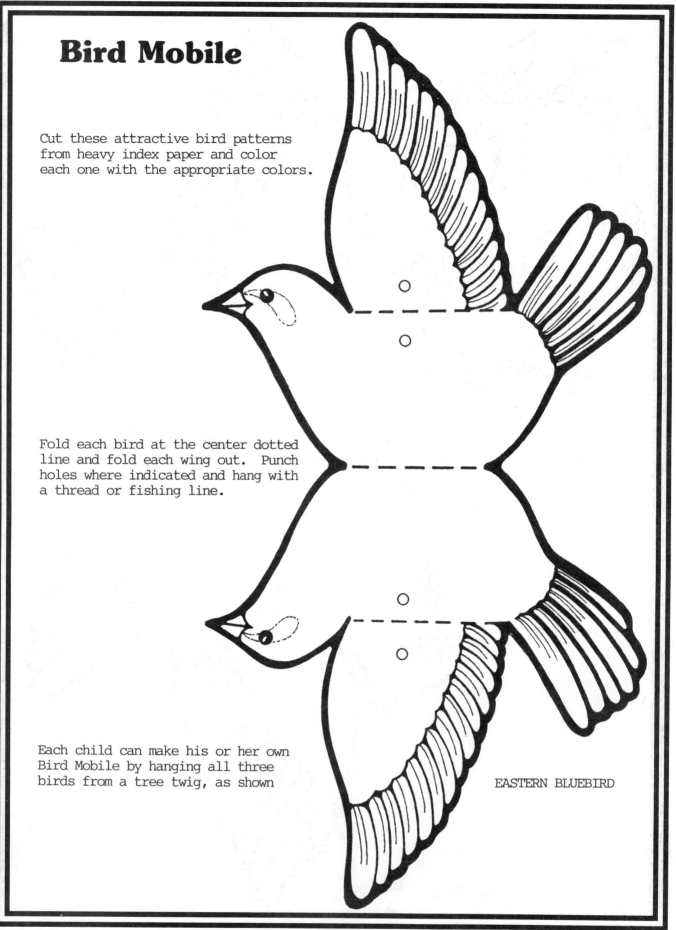

Cut these attractive bird patterns from heavy index paper and color each one with the appropriate colors.

Fold each bird at the center dotted line and fold each wing out. Punch holes where indicated and hang with a thread or fishing line.

Each child can make his or her own Bird Mobile by hanging all three birds from a tree twig, as shown

EASTERN BLUEBIRD

CARDINAL

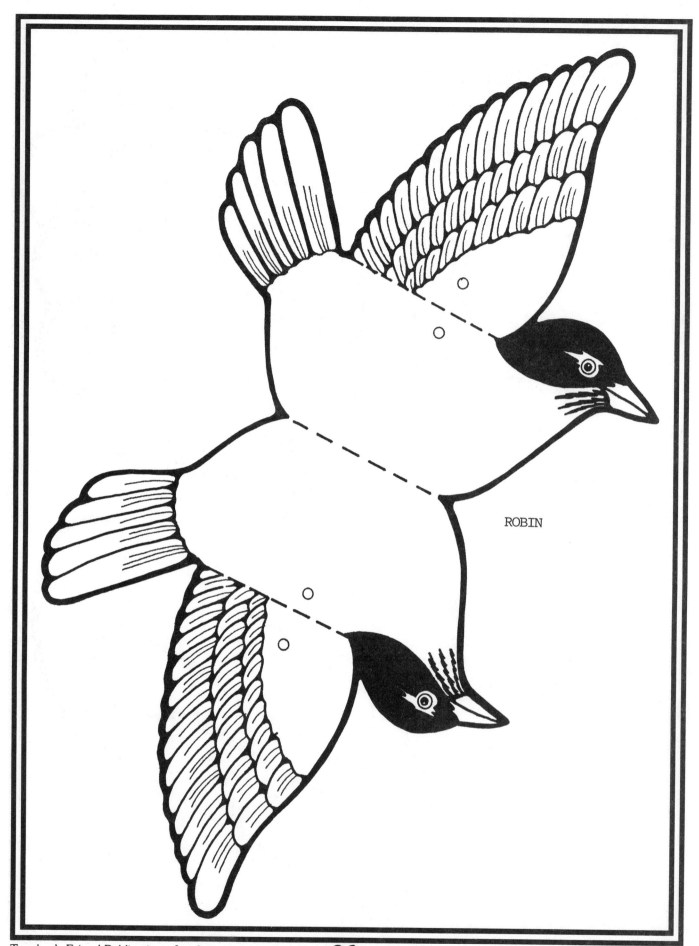

ROBIN

May Fun Glasses

Cut the pattern pieces from heavy index paper and color with markers or crayons. Attach the bows to the frame by fitting them into the designated slots.

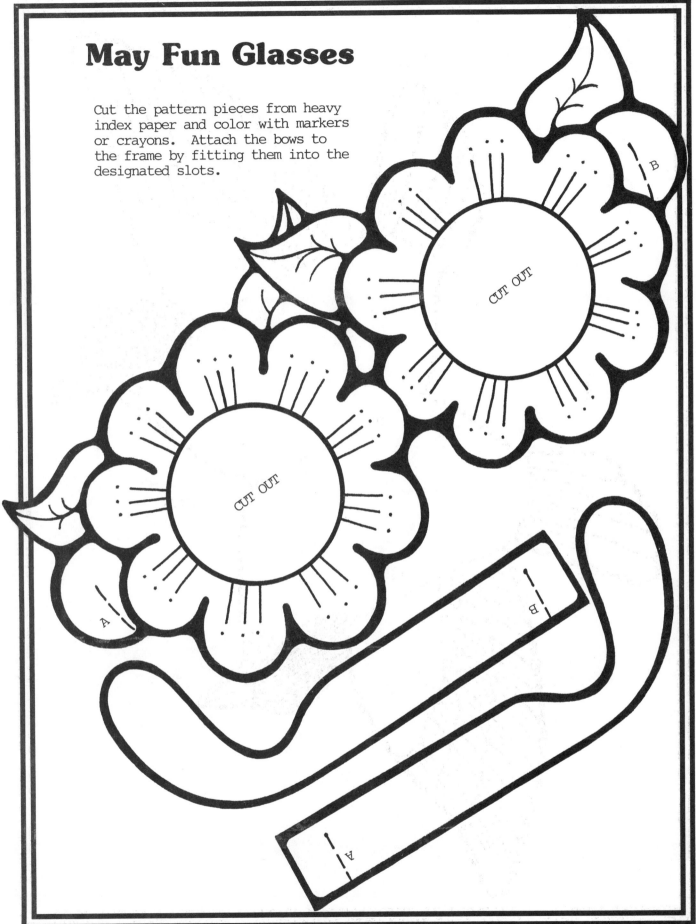

Stand-Up Flowers

Cut out this cute character and flowers from heavy paper. Write your own message across the flowers. Fan fold along the dotted lines. Glue the character to the first flower and stand on a desk or use as a Mother's Day card.

Mother's Day Activities

A CHILD'S VIEW OF MOTHER'S DAY

When I am big and old and grown,
I will have children of my own.
I'll have a great big rocking chair
And rock them while I'm sitting there.

I'll teach them colors, numbers, too,
And teach them how to tie a shoe.
When they are sick, I'll make them better.
When it is cold, they'll wear a sweater.

I'll wash their socks and underwear,
And all their meals I will prepare.
And if I have a girl or boy,
I'll play the games that they enjoy.

I will buy them what they need
And I will teach them how to read.
I will teach them how to write
And I'll be sure they sleep all night.

I'll teach them how to catch a ball
And kiss their hurts, if they should fall.
For every child I'll work quite hard.
For me they'll make a Mother's Day card.

I think I'd better do that right now.
It's for my Mom. I should know how.
I'll write a card, "This is for you,
"To thank you, Mom, for all you do."

"I'm glad that now when you are grown,
I have you, Mom, my very own!"

THANK YOU MOM!

Ask children to think of ways in
which they usually forget to thank
their mothers. Have them write
their special thank you notes on
pastel colored paper and include
it in a Mother's Day card!

BABY NAMES

Most animals have specific
names for the babies. See
if your students can deter-
mine what type of animals
have these babies:

foal
cub
calf
duckling
whelp
gosling
joey
fawn
pup
kitten
chick
piglet
lamb
bunny
kid

RECIPE FOR MOM

Children will love creating "MOM"
recipes! Ask each child to write
a recipe using the ingredients that
make his or her mom special. Here
is an example:

In a large bowl combine 3 cups of
happiness and 2 pounds of love.
Gently stir together with a table-
spoon of kindness, a dash of dis-
cipline and a sprinkle of patience.
Slowly warm in a loving atmosphere
and soon you'll have something
special, my MOM!

Woven Hearts

This Woven Heart can be given to mom for a simple Mother's day gift. Fill it with small candies, notes of appreciation or wild flowers.

Cut two patterns from pastel colored construction paper. Fold each pattern in half and make three cuts down the center. Hold one piece in each hand and carefully weave the first piece in one hand over and under the piece in your other hand. Continue weaving each piece the same way. Attach a small paper handle to the top. When you are finished, your woven heart will look like the one above.

Stand-Up Mom

Make this Stand-Up Mom from index paper. Color, cut out and fold. Attach the heart to one hand and write a special message on her apron.

Stand her on a table for a Mother's Day decoration or give her as a card to your own mom on her special day!

I Love You MOM

Two, three or four children can play this game. Each player rolls a die and moves
first player to reach the finish line is the winner. Children will love discov-

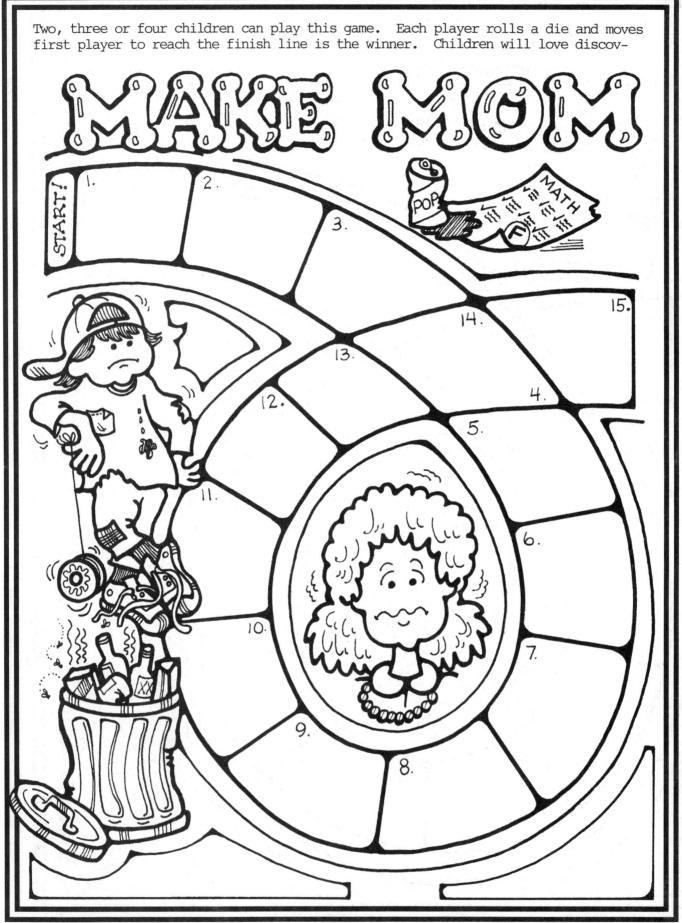

the required spaces. The player takes a task card and does what it says. The
ering ways to make mom happy!

MESSY ROOM!

LOSE A TURN

LATE FOR DINNER!

GO BACK ONE SPACE

DID NOT COMPLETE HOMEWORK!

GO BACK ONE SPACE

FORGOT TO FEED THE FAMILY PETS!

GO BACK TWO SPACES

HIT YOUR LITTLE BROTHER!

GO BACK TWO SPACES

CHEATED ON A TEST AT SCHOOL!

GO BACK THREE SPACES

FORGOT TO TAKE OUT THE GARBAGE!

LOSE A TURN

TOLD A LIE!

GO BACK THREE SPACES

CLEANED UP YOUR ROOM!

MOVE AHEAD ONE SPACE

HELPED YOUR MOTHER IN THE KITCHEN!

MOVE AHEAD ONE SPACE

TOOK OUT THE GARBAGE WITHOUT BEING ASKED!

TAKE ANOTHER TURN

TURNED IN ALL ASSIGNMENTS AT SCHOOL!

TAKE ANOTHER TURN

BROUGHT HOME A GOOD STUDENT AWARD!

MOVE AHEAD THREE SPACES

HELPED YOUR YOUNGER BROTHER WITH HIS HOMEWORK!

MOVE AHEAD THREE SPACES

SHARED A TOY WITH YOUR SISTER!

MOVE AHEAD TWO SPACES

BOUGHT A MOTHER'S DAY GIFT FOR MOM WITH YOUR OWN MONEY!

MOVE AHEAD TWO SPACES

Mother' Day Coupon Book

This clever coupon book makes a perfect Mother's Day gift.

Copy the coupons onto index paper and have students do the coloring with crayons or colored markers. Punch two holes where indicated and attach the book together with a ribbon or piece of yarn. Children can also add their own coupons using the provided blank pages.

Mother will love receiving this gift and redeeming each coupon!

Happy
Mother's Day
Coupon Book

Love,

_____

Redeem this coupon and I'll take out
the trash ___ times!

Mother's Day
Coupon Book

Redeem this coupon and I'll feed
our pets ___ times!

Mother's Day
Coupon Book

Redeem this coupon
and I'll help in
the kitchen
___ times!

Mother's Day
Coupon Book

Redeem this coupon
and I'll clean
my room
___ times!

Mother's Day
Coupon Book

TOYS

**Mother's Day
Coupon Book**

**Mother's Day
Coupon Book**

SOCCER ACTIVITIES

SOCCER CHARACTER

SOCCER BOARD GAME

SOCCER BULLETIN BOARDS

CREATIVE WRITING SOCCER BALLS

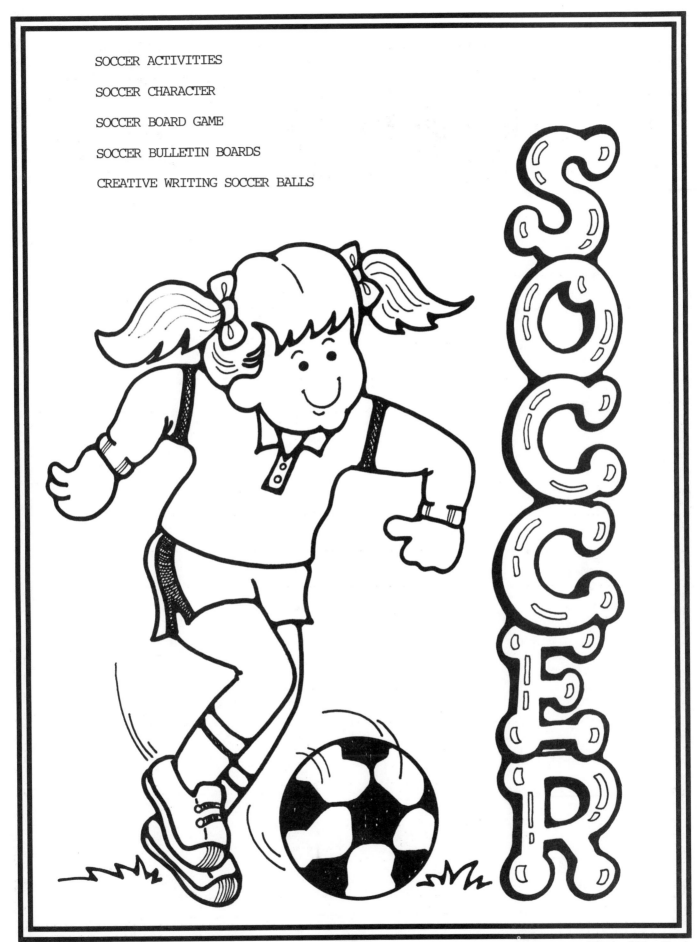

Soccer Activities

SOCCER

The point of the game is the ball to the goal.
Each team wants the ball in its own control.
Most of the game is a run and a kick.
Players legs must be active and strong and quite quick.

Don't use your hands, just feet instead.
You may use your shoulders, you may use your head.
You may kick with your heels, insteps and toes
To score a big win against the team you oppose.

You may kick with your left foot and also your right.
Be sure your shoes are laced firmly and tight.
One thing you don't ever want to do
Is kick the ball and then off comes your shoe!

Soccer Bingo

This game offers an exciting way to introduce students to soccer vocabulary words. Give each child a copy of the bingo words listed below or write the words on the chalkboard. Ask students to write any 24 words on his or her bingo cards. Use the same directions you might use for regular bingo.

(Students might like to use some of these words in a creative writing assignment.)

SOCCER	PENALTY AREA	FIELD	DEFENDER
FOOTBALL	KICK	CHAMPION	MIDFIELDER
GOAL	STRIKERS	FOUL	FORWARD
PERIOD	WINGS	THROW-IN	NET
TEAM	LINKSMEN	WALL	CHARGING
GOALIE	STOPPER	BALL	CHEST TAP
PENALTY	SWEEPER	OLYMPICS	THIGH TAP
TOUCHLINES	PENALTY ZONE	INTERNATIONAL	FOOT TAP
CENTER CIRCLE	SAVE	SCORE	HEAD TAP
GOAL AREA	REFEREE	POINTS	PLAYER

SOCCER BINGO

FREE

KICK FOR

TEACHERS: Make your own task cards for this game that two, three or four children can play.

THE GOAL!

Soccer Character

Make this cute character from index paper. Color, cut out and fold. Bend his arms forward and staple or paste the ball to his hands.

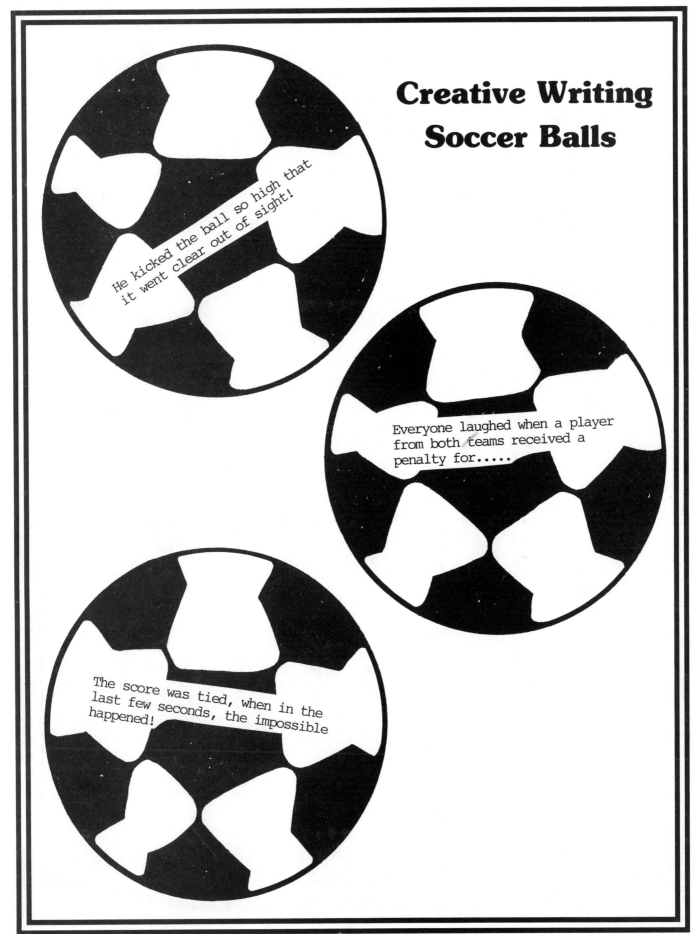

Creative Writing
Soccer Balls

He kicked the ball so high that it went clear out of sight!

Everyone laughed when a player from both teams received a penalty for.....

The score was tied, when in the last few seconds, the impossible happened!

Soccer Bulletin Boards

GOALS FOR THE FUTURE!

Motivate your students to examine their future goals with this easy bulletin board. Enlarge these cute soccer characters with an overhead projector and display them on the board. Children can write poems or creative stories about their goals for the next school year or occupations they may wish to have when they are grown.

KICK-OFF FACTS!

Children can review their multiplication tables with this simple bulletin board. Display a large soccer ball made from black and white construction paper. Write multiplication problems on each section of the ball. As a class, review the answers after the students have worked the problems at their desks.